# A Rainbow of Recipes

## A Colorful Cookbook for Kids

### Cook, Craft, Create

*Donna Castelluccio*

*Once Upon A Thyme*

2001

Cooking is as much fun and as creative
as making mud pies.

Cooking is trying this and that,
experimenting, like science.

Cooking is measuring, halving, and
doubling, like math.

Cooking is great taste, wonderful
aroma's and visually appealing.

Share the fun and double the pleasure!

# CONTENTS

# KITCHEN CAUTIONS

A parent should be supervising in the kitchen.

Be careful with knives, get help.

Be aware of hot objects – use caution – use pot holders and oven mitts

Steam is hot! Do not put face or hands near boiling water.

Make sure pot handles face in and do not hang over to get knocked off.

Be sure to turn off the stove when done.

Make sure the blender is covered before using.

Use organic fruits and veggies or wash really well.

When using edible flowers be sure it is edible, identified correctly and organic.

Clean up after yourself!

Don't be afraid to experiment.

Have Fun!

Be safe!

# GLOSSARY

Boil – to bubble over direct heat

Broil – expose directly to intense heat

Chop -to cut into small pieces

Cream – to soften a fat, like butter, beating it at room temperature. Butter and sugar are often creamed to make a smooth, creamy paste.

Dice- to cut into very small pieces

Grate – to grind into shreds or particles by rubbing or scraping

Infuse – to soak to extract flavors

Marinate – to soak in a solution (usually oil, wine, vinegar and spices) before cooking to tenderize and flavor

Meld – the flavors come together, blend, merge

Mince – to chop into very small bits

Puree – to mash foods together by hand or blender to make smooth textured

Sautee – to cook food quickly in a small amount of hot shortening

Simmer – to cook in liquid just below the boiling point, when tiny bubbles form on the surface.

Steep – to immerse in liquid in order to extract or to enhance flavor, like tea in hot water.

# RED

# Jazzy Red Tea

1tsp. jasmine flowers

1 C. water

Put the jasmine in a tea cup, tea ball or heat seal tea bag. Pour the cup of boiling water over the herb. Let it <u>steep</u> for 3-5 minutes. Watch it turn red. Great taste and smell. Serve hot or cold (iced tea). Add milk, sugar, honey or lemon as usual.

Lots of herbs can be used to make tea. The rule is 1 tsp. of dried herb or 1 Tbs. fresh to 1 C. of boiling water. Let <u>steep</u> 5-10 minutes.

*Herbs to use: lemon balm, lemon verbena, mint, sage, thyme, rosemary, bee balm, rose hips, roses, lavender flowers, chamomile flowers, scented geranium leaves, anise hyssop, pineapple sage.*

1 serving

# Purple Basil Vinegar

Clean, dry jar and lid - any size

Purple basil leaves, fresh! - clean and <u>dry</u> (any water will cloud the vinegar and the herbs will mold).

White vinegar

Fill jar loosely with purple basil, pour vinegar over until covered. Let <u>steep</u> for 2 weeks. Comes out a pretty red color. Tasty too!

Variations: Add oregano, parsley, basil, thyme and chives.

Using the same method for an orange color, orange nasturtium flowers (peppery taste)

Use vinegar as a salad dressing, alone or mixed with oil. Add to

soups, potato salad, coleslaw (page 54), stew, even drizzle on a sandwich.

# Bar-B-Q sauce

1C catsup

½ C vinegar

3 Tbs chopped onion (more or less to taste)

2 Tbs Worchester sauce

4 Tbs brown sugar

½ tsp dry mustard

¼ - ½ C chopped herbs fresh or 2-4 Tbs dried

Try basil, parsley, oregano, chives, garlic, cilantro,

sage, thyme,

fennel, dill, savory, marjoram

Mix altogether and put it in a clean, dry bottle.

Let flavors blend at least 2 week before using.

Keep refrigerated

# Salsa

2C diced tomatoes – any kind and combination

¼ C bell pepper diced

1 Tbs chopped onion

1 Tbs finely chopped jalapeno pepper

1 Tbs fresh cilantro chopped

1 clove garlic minced

Salt and pepper to taste

1 Tbs lime juice

1 Tbs olive oil

Combine and serve

Jalapeno peppers are hot, use sparingly (or not!). **When handling hot pepper keep your hands away from you face. Wash your hands well after handling hot peppers.

Be careful chopping! Get help from an adult.

# Spiced Cranberry Sauce

12 oz. cranberries

1 C. sugar*

1 C. orange juice

1 tsp. dried rosemary, crushed

In a saucepan over med. heat dissolve the sugar in the OJ.

Stir in cranberries and cook until skin opens, about 5-10 min.

Stir in rosemary and remove from heat. Cool.

Other herbs that can be used: cinnamon & cloves, mint, any lemon herb.

To crush rosemary use a mortar and pestle, blender or coffee grinder until fine.

*Use a flavored sugar, vanilla, mint, lavender – recipe pgs. 52 & 53.

# Chili

1 lb ground beef or turkey

1 chopped onion (more or less to taste – optional)

1 clove garlic chopped

½ C green pepper, chopped

8 oz can red kidney beans

8 oz tomato sauce

2 tsp chili powder

1 bay leaf

Saute, in a large pot, meat, onions, garlic and pepper over med high heat, until meat is browned. Add beans, sauce, chili powder and bay leaf.

Simmer for one hour. Serve topped with sour cream,

grated/shredded cheddar or Monterey Jack cheese. Corny muffins from page 33 make a great side dish. Serves 4

**Grinnell Public Library**
2642 East Main Street
Wappingers Falls, NY 12590
www.Grinnell-Library.org

# Rose and Milk Bath

This is the bath said to make Cleopatra young and beautiful.

Roses are hydrating- they add water to the skin which helps prevent wrinkles- you may not worry about this now but remember the tip. The milk softens the skin and makes it glow.

It was said Cleopatra filled the tub with milk. You can if it's okay with the adult, but it might be better to try this recipe.

1/2 C. dried whole milk powder

1/2 C. dried roses

Tie these up in a washcloth, large heat sealable tea bag or in a muslin culinary bag.

Toss in the tub. Inhale the wonderful fragrance and run the bag over your skin.

This is a one time use- make several.

Do not use the roses loose - they will clog the drain!

# ORANGE

# Hot Spiced Cider

4 C. apple cider

4- 6" cinnamon sticks

10 cloves

6 allspice

lemon rind

Simmer all the ingredients together in a pot on the stove for about 20 minutes for the flavors to blend.  Serve warm, strain out the spices.

Serves 4

# **Infused** Honey

1 cup honey

4 star anise

4 cinnamon sticks

6 cloves

Vanilla bean

Warm ingredients in a saucepan over medium-low heat for 5 to 10 minutes. Turn off heat and put into clean, dry jar. Let rest for at least 30 minutes or overnight. Serve over hot cereal, in tea, over pancakes or just lick the spoon.

Variations: Place any one of these herbs on the bottom of a clean, dry jar: 1/2 vanilla bean, 3 rose scented geranium leaves, 4 thyme sprigs, 2 lavender sprigs or 1 Tbs. dried flowers, or 2 Tbs. fresh rose petals or 1 Tbs. dried. Warm the honey then pour it over the herb in the jar. Let the flavors meld for 1 week.

Honey is great for sore throats and the addition of cinnamon is even more beneficial.

# Stuffed Nasturtium Flowers

Nasturtium flowers – organic – assorted colors

recipe for cheese balls (page 43) - without coating

OR plain cream cheese

Pick whole, perfect, organically grown flowers and

clean gently.  Put the cheese mix into the flower
carefully so it doesn't rip.  Pop in your mouth as an

appetizer.  This looks beautiful arranged on a platter for
company.

# Pumpkin Pancakes

Makes about 16 pancakes

2 cups all-purpose flour

2 tablespoons firmly packed brown sugar

1 tablespoon baking powder

1 teaspoon salt

1 teaspoon ground cinnamon

1/4 teaspoon ground nutmeg

1/4 teaspoon ground ginger

1 1/2 cups milk

1/2 cup  pumpkin

1 large egg

2 tablespoons vegetable oil

1. In large bowl, combine dry ingredients.  In a small bowl, combine milk, pumpkin, egg, and oil; stir into flour mixture until dry ingredients are moistened.  Batter will be thick.

2. Heat lightly oiled griddle until a drop of water sizzles on the surface.

3. For each pancake, pour 1/4 cup batter onto hot griddle.

When the top bubbles, turn; cook until the bottom is golden.

Serve with infused honey – page 19.

Grow and cook your own pumpkin for a real treat!

# Pumpkin Basics

### How to Cook Pumpkin

Choose a med. size pumpkin to get the most pulp and taste. Wash the shell well. Have an adult cut the pumpkin into at least 4 slices. Using a large spoon scoop out the strings and seeds from the 'meat' of the pumpkin. Keep the seeds separate. Lay the pumpkin slices face down, shell up on greased roasting pan. Put a little water in the pan. Bake at 375, 45 min. to 1 hour, until soft.

When done and cooled scoop the pulp out from the shell and put it into a blender. Blend until smooth. If it is too thick you may need to blend it in several small batches. This is now the equivalent of canned pumpkin and can be used in recipes. I freeze leftovers in 1 C. amts. to use later. Do not freeze longer than 6 mos.

### Pumpkin Seeds

Try to clean off the seeds as much as possible. Rinse in cold water. Spread on a baking sheet. Season with salt. Want to try something different? Season with garlic powder or chili seasoning. Experiment with any flavors you might enjoy. Bake at 350 about 15 min. Until lightly browned. Watch carefully, do not burn.

# Carrot Soup

6 carrots- washed, scraped and cut up

4 C. chicken broth

1 tsp. soy sauce

1 tsp. ginger

1/4 tsp. pepper

sprinkle garlic powder

Simmer carrots in chicken broth until soft. Carrots are soft when a fork goes into it easily. Place carrots in food processor with a little of the liquid- puree and return to pan. Add soy, ginger, pepper and garlic. Heat and serve.

Can be served topped with sour cream and chives

Serves 4-6

# Whipped Sweet Potatoes

4 sweet potatoes- peeled cut into pieces

2 tsp. brown sugar

1 Tbs. butter or margarine

1/4 tsp. nutmeg

In a pot, cover the potatoes with water and boil until

soft- the smaller the pieces the faster it will cook.

When soft, drain water

Mash potatoes with fork, masher, or food processor

Add sugar, butter, and nutmeg

Mash and serve.

Serves 4

# Twice Baked Potatoes

4 lg. baking potatoes

3/4 C. shredded cheddar cheese

salt & pepper to taste

1/2 Tbs. parsley

1 tsp. thyme

opt. bacon bits, sour cream and chives &/or

baked beans, chili

Heat oven to 400. Wash potatoes and pierce with a fork in 3 places. Place in oven and cook 1 hour. To check if it's done stick it with a fork, if it goes in easy it's done. If it's still hard continue to cook until soft. When cool enough to handle scoop out potato from skin and put in a bowl. Add cheddar cheese, salt, pepper and parsley, mix well. Place the stuffing back in the skins. Place on a cookie sheet then into the oven again for about 15min. or until cheese melts. Top with bacon bits, sour cream & chives, chili or baked beans. Serves 4

## Salmon with Herbed Mustard Sauce

2 salmon steaks

1 Tbs. mustard (any kind)

1 tsp lemon juice

1 tsp. dry or 1 Tbs. fresh lemon grass, balm, verbena or thyme (chopped)

1/4 tsp. crushed fennel seed (or top with fresh fennel sprigs)

Mix mustard with lemon juice and herbs. Spread thinly on fish.

Broil or barbecue fish, about 15 min. Done when fish flakes easily.

Serves 4

# O-Yo Pops

3/4 cup Orange Juice

1/4 cup plain yogurt

1/2 tsp fresh mint leaves- spearmint, gingermint,
pineapplemint

OR 1/4 tsp dried mint leaves- chopped fine

Blend all together and freeze in ice pop trays until hard.

Can be frozen in ice cube trays.  Then put in blender

and serve in bowl with a sprig of mint.  Serves 1

Instead of mint try rosemary- crushed or ground

If you like licorice use anise hyssop or sweet cicely
leaves chopped

Any of the lemon herbs would be good - balm, verbena,
thyme

# POMANDER BALL

To make a pomander ball use a firm, thin skinned fruit. Oranges are the most popular but apples, lemons, kumquats, and others can be used. Stick the whole cloves, pointy end, into the fruit, if they do not go in easily you can use a pin to start the hole. The whole fruit does not need to be covered, experiment with different patterns (spirals and stripes).

The pomander then gets rolled in a spice mix both for preservation and scent.

To make the spice mix combine 4 oz. cinnamon, 2 oz. cloves, 1/2 oz. allspice, 1/2 oz. nutmeg and 1 oz. powdered orris root

Hang to dry in a mesh bag or netting in a dry, airy place. The fruit will shrink as it dries. Tie it with ribbons and hang or display several in a bowl.

The pomander became popular during the Middle Ages when the black death and other ailments ran rampant. The streets and even some homes were strewn with filth, bodily fluids and the discarded remnants of past meals. The belief went that the pleasant scent of a pomander could repel the disease in the air. It was used for scent and to ward off disease.

# YELLOW

# Lemonade with a twist

## Rose lemonade

1 C lemon juice (about 4 lemons)

2 ½ C cold water

½ C rosewater

½ C sugar

Mix all together. Add ice cubes and chill.

*Rose petals can be added to the ice tray before freezing – looks good.

*Put rose petals in the pitcher.

## Lavender lemonade

1 C lemon juice

2 C water

1 C lavender tea – cooled

½ C sugar

To make lavender tea – 1 tsp dried lavender or 4 fresh lavender spikes to 1 C boiling water. Simmer 5 min. Strain out lavender.

You can use powdered lemonade mix substituting rose water or lavender tea for some of the water required.

# **Herbed Butter**

1 stick of butter or margarine

2 Tbs fresh herb or 1 Tbs dried – use 1 or more herbs
chives, tarragon, basil, thyme, parsley, nasturtium
(peppery), sage, rosemary

optional: 1 clove minced garlic or hot pepper to taste

You can use prepared herb mixes like bouquet garni

( pg.41)

Use on rolls, rice, veggies, pasta, corn on the cob

*substitute cream cheese for the butter

# Grilled Corn on the Cob

1 ear of corn

Butter or margarine melted (optional)

fresh herbs like: mint, thyme, basil, lemon verbena, tarragon

Soak the corn in water for 15 min. Peel the corn husk down and remove the silks but not the husk. Brush the corn lightly with butter and put the herb leaves on. Pull the husk up around the ear. Place on a hot grill for about 10 min, turn after 5 min.

# CORNY MUFFINS

1 C flour

½ C yellow cornmeal

1/3 C sugar

1 Tbs baking powder

¼ tsp salt

1 C corn – fresh, canned or frozen (defrost)

2 eggs

½ C milk

½ C margarine melted

½ tsp dried red pepper

1 tsp dry or 1 Tbs fresh parsley

Preheat oven to 400. Mix all dry ingredients together. Add corn to the dry mix to coat the corn. Beat the eggs in a separate bowl. Add milk and margarine to the eggs and mix well. Add the wet ingredients to the dry ingredients, mix until blended. Grease muffin tin and fill 2/3 full. Bake 15-20 min.

Goes great with Chili (pg 15)

# CORN SOUP

3 Tbs butter (opt.use herbed pg 31)

3 cloves garlic minced

3 C corn

2 ½ C milk

1 Tbs dried or 3 Tbs fresh thyme

1 tsp salt

Pepper to taste

Red pepper (cayenne) to taste

¼ C chopped chives (optional topping)

Melt butter in a large saucepan. Add the garlic and cook over medium heat stirring occasionally until soft. Stir in corn, milk and seasonings. Bring to a simmer and cook until soup thickens, about 15 min, stir occasionally.

Serve garnished with the chives.

# SUNRISE EGGS

4 eggs

¼ c grated cheddar cheese or 4 slices yellow
American cheese

A dash of salt, pepper and tarragon


Preheat oven to 325. Crack the eggs into an oven proof glass or Pyrex dish. Try not to break the yolk but if you do it tastes the same, no big deal. Sprinkle the herbs over the eggs. Spread the cheese evenly over the top. Bake the eggs uncovered for 15 min., just until firm.

# YELLOW RICE

2 C water

1 C white rice

¼ tsp saffron

½ C raisins (optional)

Put the water in a saucepan. Put the heat on high.

Add the saffron to the water. When the water boils

add the rice.

Cover and lower the heat so it simmers. Simmer 20 min.

When the water is absorbed and the rice is soft it is done.

Add the raisins if desired. Add a little butter and enjoy .

*Saffron is one of the most expensive spices. It comes from the flower of the saffron crocus. The saffron threads are the stigma of the flower.

# <u>Curry</u>

6 Tbs dried coriander - ground

1 1/2 Tbs ground turmeric

1 1/2 Tbs cumin

11/2 Tbs ground fenugreek

11/2 tsp. cloves

11/2 tsp. ground cardamon

dash cayenne

Mix ground spices all together. Store in airtight jar, label.

Use in curry kabobs (pg. 38).

If you have whole spices use a mortar and pestle, coffee grinder or blender to grind.

Curry is an Indian spice blend. It can be used on chicken (next page), rice, cheese balls (page 43), lamb.

# Curry Kabobs

1 lb. chicken cutlets

3/4 C. mayo

1/2 C. sour cream

1 Tbs fresh parsley (1tsp. dried)

1 tsp lemon juice

1/2 tsp. Worchester sauce

1 tsp grated onion

salt and pepper to taste

1/4 tsp curry powder (page 37)

Mix all the ingredients except chicken and chill.

Let flavors blend at least 1/2 hr. Cut chicken into bite size pieces. Put on shish kabob skewers. Brush the chicken with the sauce and barbecue or broil about 30 min, turning occasionally.

Reapply sauce toward the middle to end of cooking.

variations: Marinate the chicken for 1 hour in the curry sauce.

Use the sauce for dipping chunks of chicken, beef, lamb.

Serves 4-6

# FALL POTPOURRI

4 small sunflower heads

6 dried orange slices

Dried lemon peel

½ C calendula flowers

1 C chamomile flowers

6- 6" cinnamon sticks

¼ C cloves

1 C bay leaves

¼ C orris root

30 drops bergamot essential oil

Put the orris root in a paper cup and add the bergamot oil and mix. Mix everything else together in a large bowl, except sunflowers. Add the orris mix. Display potpourri in a basket or bowl. Decorate the top with the sunflowers.

The orris root acts as a fixing agent so the scent lasts longer.

To dry orange and lemon peels – peel the fruit. Leave the skin on a paper towel in a sunny area. Depending on humidity it should be done in 1 day.

Dry orange slices – Cut the orange into thin slices. Put on a baking sheet in the oven on the lowest setting until dry but not brown. If you have a dehydrator this works well.

# GREEN

# BOUQUET GARNI

This is a seasoning to use in soups, sauces or stews. It is a very popular French blend.

1/4 oz.parsley

1 bay leaf - broken in pieces

1/2 oz. thyme

1/2 oz. marjoram

1/2 oz. rosemary

Sage, savory and basil can be substitutes or additions.

Mix these together and put about 1 Tbs. per muslin bag, cheesecloth or heat seal tea bag. Fresh herbs can be used but double the amount. Tie sprigs of the fresh herbs together with lemon grass and use that way.

# DILLY DIP

11/3 C. mayonnaise

11/2 C. sour cream

2 Tbs. parsley

2 Tbs. minced onion

2 Tbs. dill weed

large round loaf of Italian bread

Mix the first five ingredients together and refrigerate.
An adult must help cutting the bread. Cut off the
top and scoop out the soft part of the bread. Leave
only the crust as a shell.
Cut the bread that was removed into bite size
pieces and arrange it on a plate around the
bread shell. Pour the dip into the shell and dip
in the cut pieces of bread.
This is my family's favorite!

# Cheese Balls

2 c softened cream cheese

1/4 c cheddar cheese grated

1/2 Tsp. prepared mustard powder

1 Tbs. softened butter

2 Tbs. fresh herbs or 1 Tbs. dry

parsley, thyme, sage, or dill are good choices

(use 1herb or a mix)

1/4 Tsp. pepper

1-2 cloves minced garlic

Using a wooden spoon blend all the ingredients together until well mixed. Form into 1" balls.

Coating

red- paprika, cayenne (if you like hot), chili powder

green- chopped parsley, dill, chives, tarragon

yellow - curry (page 37)

Place about 2 Tbs. of selected coating in a bowl. Roll the cheese balls in the herb until well coated. Serve as horsdeuvers.

Needs to be refrigerated

Red and green - great for Christmas!

# GREEN SALAD

Lettuce leaves – any and all varieties

Peppers – cut up

Green beans

Peas

Cucumbers – round slices

Chives – chopped


Leaves of herbs such as; mint, basil, lemon balm, oregano, parsley, dill, thyme, salad burnet borage and nasturtium leaves & flowers (edible!)


Wash all greens. Cut or chop as desired and toss together.

Use your favorite dressing or

Oil & purple basil vinegar (pg 11)

# Zucchini Crunchies

## 2 medium zucchini

## 4 Tbs. Italian salad dressing (not creamy)

## 2 Tbs bread crumbs

## 2 Tbs. grated parmesan cheese

## 1 tsp. garlic powder

Preheat oven to 475 degrees. Lightly grease cookie sheet.

Slice zucchini into spears. Put the dressing in a shallow bowl. Combine the bread crumbs, parmesan and garlic in another bowl. Dip the zucchini in the dressing and then roll in bread crumb mix. Place on baking sheet in single layer. Bake uncovered 5 minutes then turn and bake 4 more minutes.

Serves 4

Flowers of zucchini are edible! See stuffed nasturtiums pg 20

# Green Bean Supreme

1 1lb. can wax beans

1 1lb. can cut green beans

1 1lb. can chick peas

1 8oz. can black olives - <u>chopped</u>

1/2 C. chopped chives

1/2 C. <u>minced</u> green pepper

1/2 C. oil

1/3 C. red wine vinegar

1/4 C. red wine

1/2 C. sugar

1/4 tsp garlic powder

1/4 tsp. basil

Drain the liquid from the cans. Combine the beans, olives, onions and pepper in a bowl. In a separate bowl mix the oil, vinegar, wine, sugar and herbs. Pour this over the beans and refrigerate for several hours before serving.

# Pesto

3 C. fresh basil leaves

3/4 C. olive oil

2 cloves garlic

3 Tbs. Pine nuts (walnuts can be substituted)

3/4 C. parmesan cheese

Wash basil leaves and pat dry with paper towel. Place in food processor or blender. Add oil, garlic, nuts and cheese. Process. You may need to scrape down sides. Process until smooth.

Use on pasta. My favorites: spaghetti and tortellini

Use leftover pesto as a spread.

*Cut a loaf of Italian bread in half lengthwise and generously coat with the pesto. Now broil until golden, about 3-4 mins. Watch- do not burn!

*Put on crescent rolls - spread, roll up and bake per package instructions.

*Put under skin of chicken and bake

Pesto means an herb paste. Instead of basil you can substitute rosemary, parsley or tarragon. Even mix and match.

Pesto can be frozen. Nice treat mid winter!

# Marbled Green Quiche

1 Tbs butter or margarine

1 C minced onion (optional)

1 10 oz pkg frozen spinach, cooked

1 15 oz container ricotta

2 eggs

Salt & pepper to taste

¼ tsp nutmeg

1/2 C parmesan cheese

1 pie crust

Cook spinach per directions, thoroughly drain – squeeze out as much water as possible.

Melt butter, fry onion until soft. Add spinach, stir until most of the moisture is gone.

Remove from heat

In large bowl add all the other ingredients to the spinach and stir.

Pour into baked pie shell. Bake 350, about 40 min, until top golden and filling set

# Simmering Potpourri

½ C dried lavender flowers

1 C eucalyptus leaves

1 C dried thyme

Mix together. Use about ¼ C of the mix to about 2 C water. Simmer on the stove. Smells great and is antiseptic, it will clear the air of germs.

# BIV

# Herbal Purple Cow

5 oz. milk

3 oz purple grape juice

1/2 tsp. vanilla

2 ice cubes

Whirl it all in the blender and drink.

options: 1/2 tsp. mint or rosemary, chopped

1 serving

# BLUEBERRY MUFFINS

2 C flour

½ C sugar*

1 Tbs baking powder

¼ tsp salt

1 egg

1 C milk

¼ C oil

1 C blueberries

Preheat oven to 400. Lightly grease muffin tin.

Mix dry ingredients in a bowl. Toss in the berries and coat.

In a small bowl beat egg with a fork. Stir in milk and oil.

When mixed add the wet ingredients to the dry. Stir until moistened. Fill muffin tins ¾. Bake approximately 20 min. until center is dry.

Options

- *use vanilla sugar in place of sugar (recipe below)
- Add fresh lemon balm or lemon verbena – 2 Tbs chopped
- Add 1 tsp cinnamon or cardamon

Vanilla sugar – Place 1 whole vanilla bean in a quart jar (clean, dry) Pour sugar over the bean, cover and let stand 1 month for the flavors to meld. Use in any recipe as a sugar substitute for more flavor.

# LAVENDER MUFFINS

2 C flour

1/3 C lavender sugar (recipe at end)

3 tsp baking powder

½ tsp salt

1 egg

¾ C milk

½ C oil

Preheat oven to 400. Lightly grease muffin tin

Mix dry ingredients in a bowl.

In a small bowl beat egg with a fork. Stir in milk and oil. When mixed add the wet ingredients to the dry. Stir until moistened.

Fill muffin tins ¾. Bake approximately 20 min., until center is dry.

## Lavender sugar

¼ C dried lavender buds, finely ground

¾ C sugar

Combine the ingredients in a clean, dry jar. Cover and set aside for 2 weeks to blend the flavors. Use in recipes to replace regular sugar. Try it in pies, cakes and cookies.

# Purple Slaw

3 C. shredded red cabbage

1/2 C. grated red onion (more or less to taste)

1/3 C. mayo

1 Tbs. herb vinegar (or try pickle juice!)

1 tsp. dill weed, caraway or celery seed

The easiest way to shred cabbage is in a food processor but you can use a grater - watch your fingers! Mix everything together until blended. Serve now or refrigerate.

# Blueberry Syrup

1 C. blueberries

1/3 C. honey (use the infused honey, page 19)

1/4 C. water

1/2 tsp. vanilla

optional - sprinkle with cinnamon

Put berries in saucepan and crush with the back of a wooden spoon. Add honey and water and boil. Cook about 10 minutes until thickened. Add vanilla, stir.

Use on pancakes, waffles, yogurt, ice-cream.

Try with any berry.

# Glitter Grapes

purple grapes (can be any color grapes!)

1 egg white

2 Tbs. water

sugar (can be flavored - vanilla or mint or try Jello powder!)

Beat the egg whites and water in a bowl with a fork. Put the sugar in a shallow dish. Roll the grapes in the egg mix and then roll in sugar. Let dry on wax paper and then pop in your mouth for a great snack or arrange in a bowl. Freeze them and try it that way.

**How to separate an egg -**

To separate whites and yolks by hand, crack the egg open by tapping the center on the edge of a glass bowl. Hold the egg upright over the bowl and slowly separate the halves, keeping the white and yolk in one half. Then, pour the yolk into the other half, letting the white drop out. Keep moving the yolk back and forth until all of the white is in the bowl.

# BIV Jam Cookies

## Dry ingredients:

1 C. flour

1 C. raw almonds (or walnuts, pecans)

1C. oatmeal (uncooked)

1/4 tsp. cinnamon

1/4 tsp salt

## Wet ingredients

1/2 C. oil             1/4 tsp. almond extract

1/2 C. maple syrup     1/2 tsp. vanilla ext.

grape, elderberry, blueberry or plum jam (biv)

Preheat oven to 375. In food processor, blend oats and nuts, not too fine. Combine all dry ingredients in a bowl. Combine wet ingredients in food processor and whirl. Add the wet to the bowl of dry and mix well. Grease cookie sheets. Roll dough into 1" balls and place on cookie sheet. Using your thumb put a dent in the center of each cookie and fill with about 1/2 tsp. of jam. Bake 15-20 min, until brown.

apricot jam - yellow

orange marmalade - orange

strawberry or raspberry jam - red

# BLUEBERRY GRAHAM SQUARES

My mother's specialty (she didn't have many!)

18 graham crackers - crushed

1/4 C. powdered sugar

1/4 C. margarine - melted

2 eggs - beaten

1/2 C. sugar*

8 oz. cream cheese, softened

1 can blueberry pie filling

1 lemon- juiced

cinnamon if desired

Preheat oven to 350. Mix the graham crackers, powdered sugar and margarine, then spread in greased 9x13 pan. Beat the eggs, add sugar and cream cheese, blend well. Pour over the crust.

Bake 20 minutes or until brown. Cool. Combine

the pie filling and lemon and pour on top. Sprinkle with cinnamon if you want. Top with whipped cream. Cut into squares.

*Use a flavored sugar, mint, vanilla, lavender

# LAVENDER SACHET

Lavender flowers – dried

Material

ribbon

Glue

There are many ways to make a sachet, easy to hard. They can be filled with any scented flower; lavender, roses, or potpourri. You can also use essential oils by adding them to cornstarch to get the desired scent.

Easy:

Buy culinary or muslin bags and fill with scented items. This bag can be decorated first with markers, dried flowers, ribbons and do dads.

Moderate:

Cut a 12" circle from a pretty fabric or netting (not with cornstarch!).

Place the lavender in the center and tie up the top with ribbon. Put a dried stem tied into the ribbon.

Harder:

Cut 2 pieces of pretty fabric about 4"x6". Place the fabric back to back and glue 3 sides together. Let dry. Fill the bag and glue the 4th side. Decorate it further with ribbon, lace, trim.

Hardest:

Start as above but place material pattern to pattern and sew 3 and a half sides. Turn inside out, fill with flowers and finish final sewing.

Put sachets on tables, in drawers, closets, lockers, car, luggage.

Lavender is a stress reducer so carry some in your pocket!

# RAINBOW

# RAINBOW GARDEN

<u>Red</u> – tulips*, nasturtium*', monarda (bee balm)*', roses*

<u>Orange</u> – calendula*, nasturtium*', marigolds*, poppy, daylily*

<u>Yellow</u> – sunflower*, rudbekia, zinnia, yarrow, coreopsis, dandelion*', chamomile

<u>Green</u> – rosemary*', sweet cicely*', basil*', lady's mantle, fennel*', dill*'

<u>Blue</u> – borage*', delphinium, forget-me-not, campanula, chicory*

<u>Indigo</u> – chives*', catnip, thyme*', anise hyssop*', buddleia (butterfly bush), iris

<u>Violet</u> – violets*', monarda*', lavender*, phlox, echinops

*edible flowers

' edible leaves

# RAINBOW TEA

Rose petals or rose hips

Calendula and / or orange rind

Chamomile and/or lemon rind

Rosemary and/or mint

Bee balm

Lavender

Combine ingredients in any amounts you want, add more of what you like. Put 1 tsp of mix in a tea ball for 1 cup of tea. Let brew 3-5 min. Sweeten to taste.

# CRUDITE

### (fresh veggies to dip)

Red – tomatoes, red pepper, radish

Orange – carrots, orange pepper and tomatoes

Yellow - yellow pepper, yellow tomato, yellow squash

Green – peppers, zucchini, celery, broccoli, cucumbers

Blue – borage flowers to decorate the dip

Indigo – radicchio

Violet – violet flowers to decorate

Use the dilly dip recipe (pg 42) or any favorite dip.

Vegetables come in all different colors. Browse the supermarket, farmer's market and seed catalogs for ideas. Tomatoes are not just red, peppers come in all colors and shapes. Look around.

*Colorful veggies can also be stir fried for a fun Chinese meal. Use peanut oil, soy sauce, garlic and ginger.

# CONFETTI RICE

Rice

Tomatoes, diced

Carrots, thinly sliced

Corn, cooked

Peas

Borage flowers

Purple pepper, diced

Violet flowers

Cook rice according to directions. When done toss with everything else. Fun to mix up, pretty, tasty, nutritious.

# FRUIT SALAD

Red – strawberries, raspberries

Orange – oranges, tangerines

Yellow – star fruit, banana, lemon juice

Green - Grapes , kiwi

Blue – blueberries, elderberries

Indigo – black raspberries

Herbs for flavor - add chopped leaves of any of these to the fruit salad: lemon balm, sweet cicely (licorice flavor), ground cinnamon, coconut thyme, scented geranium leaves.

# INDEX

## Drinks

## CONDIMENTS/SAUCES

## APPETIZERS

## ABOUT THE AUTHOR

Donna Castelluccio is a mother of two who spent time bonding in the kitchen. There's been some kitchen mishaps; Michelle used salt instead of sugar in a mudpie. (She also thought salt cooled off food!) Laura and a friend made a lettuce soup – we had pizza that night. Donna had an herb store where she hosted a kid's club and did some craft cooking. That's where this idea originated.

27196840R00041

Made in the USA
Charleston, SC
03 March 2014